NOTE TO PARENTS

Welcome to Kingfisher Readers! This program is designed to help young readers build skills, confidence, and a love of reading as they explore their favorite topics.

These tips can help you get more from the experience of reading books together. But remember, the most important thing is to make reading fun!

Tips to Warm Up Before Reading

- Look through the book with your child. Ask them what they notice about the pictures.
- Wonder aloud together. Ask questions and make predictions. What will this book be about? What are some words we could expect to find on these pages?

While Reading

- Take turns or read together until your child takes over.
- Point to the words as you say them.
- When your child gets stuck on a word, ask if the picture could help. Then think about the first letter too.
- Accept and praise your child's contributions.

After Reading

- Look back at the things your child found interesting. Encourage connections to other things you both know.
- Draw pictures or make models to explore these ideas.
- Read the book again soon, to build fluency.

With five distinct levels and a wealth of appealing topics, the Kingfisher Readers series provides children with an exciting way to learn to read and wonder about the world around them. Enjoy!

Ellie Costa, M.S. Ed.
Literacy Specialist, Bank Street School for Children, New York

KINGFISHER READERS

level **2**

What Animals Eat

Brenda Stones and
Thea Feldman

KINGFISHER
NEW YORK

KINGFISHER
LONDON & NEW YORK

Copyright © Kingfisher 2012
Published in the United States by Kingfisher,
175 Fifth Ave., New York, NY 10010
Kingfisher is an imprint of Macmillan Children's Books, London.
All rights reserved.

Distributed in the U.S. and Canada by Macmillan,
175 Fifth Ave., New York, NY 10010

Library of Congress Cataloging-in-Publication data
has been applied for.

Series editor: Thea Feldman
Literacy consultant: Ellie Costa, Bank St. College, New York

ISBN: 978-0-7534-6758-9 (HB)
ISBN: 978-0-7534-6759-6 (PB)

Kingfisher books are available for special promotions
and premiums. For details contact: Special Markets
Department, Macmillan, 175 Fifth Ave., New York, NY 10010.

For more information, please visit
www.kingfisherbooks.com

Printed in China
9 8 7 6 5 4 3 2 1
1TR/0811/WKT/UNTD/105MA

Picture credits
The Publisher would like to thank the following for permission to reproduce their material.
Every care has been taken to trace copyright holders. However, if there have been unintentional
omissions or failure to trace copyright holders, we apologize and will, if informed, endeavor
to make corrections in any future edition.
Top = t; Bottom = b; Center = c; Left = l; Right = r
Cover Shutterstock(SS); Pages 4 SS/Christina Richards; 5t SS/neelsky; 5b SS/Kemeo; 6 SS/Johan Swanepo
7t SS/Michael Zysman; 7b SS/Gerrit de Vries; 8 SS/David Maska; 9t SS/Ivica Jandrijevic; 9b SS/Mark
Schwettmann; 10t Alamy/Donald Mammoser; 10b SS/2009fotofriends; 11 SS/Redwood; 12 SS/Gerrit de Vries;
13 SS/Eric Gevaert; 14 Photolibrary/Gerard Soury; 15 SS/Crumpler; 16t Photolibrary/Buddy Mays;
16b SS/Wolfgang Staib; 17 SS/Dr. Morely Read; 18 SS/Monkey Business Images; 19 SS/Gusev Mikhail
Evgenivitch; 20–21 Photoshot/John Shaw/NHPA; 21 Photoshot/T. Kitchin & V. Hurst/NHPA; 22 SS/Edwin
Verin; 23 SS/Floridastock; 24 SS/NatUlrich; 27 Photolibrary/Daniel J. Cox; 29 Photolibrary/Paul Goldstein; 31
FLPA/Reinhard Dirschel.

Contents

What's for dinner?

Some animals eat plants, such as leaves, nuts, fruits, and grains.

They are called **herbivores**.

A deer is an herbivore.

Some animals eat meat.

They are called **carnivores**.

A tiger is a carnivore.

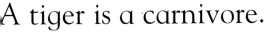

Some animals eat plants and meat.

They are called **omnivores**.

A chicken is an omnivore.

5

Elephant

What does an elephant eat?

An elephant eats grass and twigs.

It eats fruits and tree bark too.

An elephant is
an herbivore.

Giraffe

A giraffe is an herbivore too.

It reaches up, up, up.

A giraffe eats the leaves at the top of tall trees.

It reaches down to drink.

Cow

Munch, munch.

This cow chews a plant.

A cow also eats grass
and weeds.

Sheep and goats

Sheep and goats eat grass too.

They eat in the morning.

They eat in the afternoon too.

Cows, sheep, and goats are all herbivores.

Rabbit

This rabbit
nibbles grass.

What else do
rabbits eat?

Crunchy carrots
and lots of grain!

A rabbit is an herbivore.

Squirrel

Crack!

This squirrel cracks open and eats a nut.

A squirrel can also eat tree bark.

What is a squirrel?

An herbivore!

Lions

Lions eat meat.

They hunt large animals.

An animal that is hunted is called **prey**.

Lions are carnivores.

Shark

A shark is a carnivore too.

A shark eats fish
and other animals
in the sea.

Eagle

An eagle is called a **bird of prey**.

An eagle eats rabbits and snakes.

It eats fish and small birds too.

An eagle is a carnivore.

Frog

A frog eats snails, worms, and flies.

It catches prey with its sticky tongue.

A frog is a carnivore.

A baby frog only eats plants.

It is an herbivore!

Spider

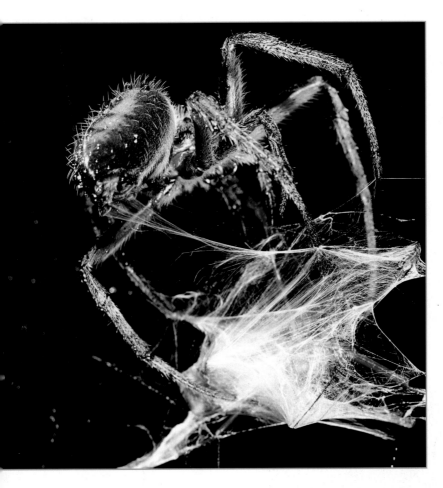

A spider spins a web to trap insects.

Then it kills and eats its prey.

A spider is a carnivore.

People

People can eat meat and plants.

People can be omnivores.

Some people do not eat meat.

Those people are called **vegetarians**

What do you eat?

Monkeys

Monkeys eat fruits, leaves, and insects.

Monkeys are omnivores.

Bears

What do bears eat?

Some bears eat fish.

Some bears eat deer or other prey.

Bears also eat berries, nuts, and grass.

Bears eat both meat and plants.

They are omnivores.

Seagulls

Seagulls are omnivores too.

They eat fish, **shellfish**, and sea plants.

Woodpecker

Tap, tap, tap!

This woodpecker
taps a hole in
the tree bark
to find ants
and beetles.

A woodpecker
eats insects.

It eats fruits,
seeds, and
nuts too.

A woodpecker
is an omnivore.

Food chains

A food chain helps us see where food comes from.

Food chains start with the Sun.

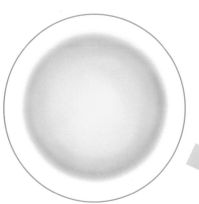

Sunlight makes
plants grow.

Some animals
eat the plants.

Bigger animals eat
smaller animals.

A food chain
in the forest

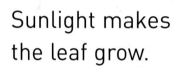

Sunlight makes
the leaf grow.

A beetle eats
the leaf.

A mouse
eats the
beetle.

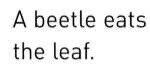

An owl eats
the mouse.

A food chain in the grasslands

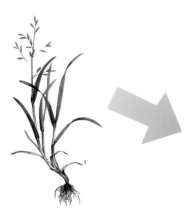

Sunlight makes the grass grow.

A zebra eats the grass.

A lion eats the zebra.

A food chain in the sea

Sunlight makes
seaweed grow.

A fish eats
the seaweed.

An octopus
eats the fish.

A shark eats the octopus.

Glossary

bird of prey a bird that kills and eats other animals

carnivores animals that eat other animals

herbivores animals that eat plants, such as leaves, fruits, nuts, and grains

omnivores animals that eat meat and plants

prey animals that are hunted for food by other animals

shellfish small sea animals with a hard shell

vegetarians people who don't eat meat

Hungry for more?
Go back through the book and look for these signs. The signs are a quick way to see what kind of "eater" everyone is!

 Herbivore

 Carnivore

 Omnivore

If you have enjoyed reading this book, look out for more in the Kingfisher Readers series!

KINGFISHER READERS: LEVEL 1

Baby Animals
Butterflies
Colorful Coral Reefs
Jobs People Do
Snakes Alive!
Trains

KINGFISHER READERS: LEVEL 2

What Animals Eat
Your Body

KINGFISHER READERS: LEVEL 3

Dinosaur World
Volcanoes

KINGFISHER READERS: LEVEL 4

Pirates
Weather

KINGFISHER READERS: LEVEL 5

Ancient Egyptians
Rainforests

For a full list of Kingfisher Readers books, plus guidance for teachers and parents and activities and fun stuff for kids, go to the Kingfisher Readers website: www.kingfisherreaders.com